I'm Forgetting Things In My Dreams

Poems by Carl Nelson

ISBN:0692638954
ISBN-13:9780692638958

DEDICATION

To everything and everyone I have forgotten or will forget - consider these poems your flowers.

Look for all these books on the Magic Bean label.

Plays by Carl Nelson:
Into the Wild Blue Yonder
Personal Growth Through Copier Sales
Ollie's Day Out

Essays by Carl Nelson:
The Audience is a Mob
The Pyramid of Rational Thought and How It Leads to Extinction

Poetry by Carl Nelson:
A Poet's Past Lives
Shoving My Way Into the Conversation
I'm Forgetting Things in My Dreams

Fiction by Eldon Cene
Murders In Progress
The Cognitive Web
The Mind Wars

All are currently available through Amazon books.

http://www.magicbeanbooks.co/home.html

CONTENTS

ACKNOWLEDGMENTS

I love to write, readers or no. But it's my wife and my son who keep me going.

MY EYE FALLS ON THIS LITTLE BIRD

While waiting in my car at Kroger's,
my eye fell on this little bird
pecking bugs from the grills of the cars around me.
'What a bright little bird,' I mused.

He couldn't have weighed more than a couple ounces.
He was not remarkable in any way;
no lovely song, dun grey feathers,
anonymous as one in a swirl of leaves.

He was quick though and fast to choose.
'It's funny I've never seen another bird
do this,' I considered,
as the bird quit the Ford and flit skyward

upwards towards the heavens.
Leaving me cast in wonder
at my own blank brain.
How vast!

OH, WHEN I DIE TO *BURN*

Enlightening this cold room
the fire heats my old hands vivid.
My toes curl outwards
flexing their soles.

Shadows flicker and mingle
among relations medieval,
a log bursting with light
and heat prickled shins.

Oh, when I die to *burn*
like that stick of wood
introducing darkness
and that glowing blush
into a woman's skin.

PAPER LANTERNS

"You're smart. Why haven't you ever used it to do some good in the world?"
- my Son

I keep hoping to draw attention
to what seems necessary.
Each day I pluck that metaphorical tin pot off the hatrack
and head out to apple the world.
Each day I pick up my pen to work
and put in several hours at the page.
Over my thoughts I sprinkle words with special seasonings.
I seal long messages to set adrift.
I release paper lanterns.

Like a bug drawn to the light,
I labor away in a very old, but honored profession.
And perhaps it's just my private issues
visiting spots of no general interest.
Nevertheless, they've been surveyed and mapped,
left rolled and stored
and marked with a big '**X**' for my son to find
should he prove adventurous.

WASHING MACHINE

This new washing machine has intelligence.
It has pauses in its thinking.
It has the 'click' of decision,
the 'thunk' of a course taken
and the grind and 'whirr' of activity.

Not one to seek a conversation,
I detail the sort of exchange I would like:
delicate, normal or heavy duty,
detail the temperature, and specify bleach and/or detergent
and finally stipulate the articles of clothing.

"Today," I say,
"we will do linens."
And that's what we do.

No matter what I load into it,
it treats them as 'linens'
and takes me at my word.
Never contradicts, never objects.

Never suggests anything
I'd rather not talk about.

OASIS

Writing on a page of white
like some parched frontiersman carving on a tree or rock
of some impassable wilderness
for some other's mind to find
has to be something.

Like the Holy Grail or a pile of gold,
a poem's strange presence has a meaning;
marks a strange yearning to where someone has troubled their way.
Some mental traveler has passed this way
willing you their campground and fire pit
with an accounting of all they found.

When you return
to the land of your birth or church
you might light them a candle
or grant them a thought.

I LIKE TO TALK WITH GOD

We have small chats
as we sit down for dinner,
little bits in between
"pass the potatoes, please."

It's rarely Biblical.
My wife takes care of that end of things.
And His Son, Jesus, rarely comes up.
Perhaps they had a falling out
or I confuse the two.

There's no dogma involved
and can take place on the front or back porches
or while the dog is walked
and pauses.
Mostly we watch the traffic whiz by
or gaze up through the trees
and take stabs at the weather.

When I say, 'chat' or 'discuss',
I mean, I do my thinking
while God is just *there.*
Actually, if He spoke
it would radically change the mood.

It must be like my dog feels resting in my lap,
or glancing up
while tinkling.

ATTENDING CHURCH

I wish attending church were more like sitting on the porch
listening to the birds chatter,
or maybe just staring at my shoes
with no one to turn at the anointed moment to say,
"The Lord be with you."

I'd rather they just turned to say,
"Hi Joe. Good to see you here this morning."
And I'd say, "Likewise."
"Wonder what the old guy is going to talk about today?"
"Don't have a clue. Hopefully, not about neither one of us."
Then I'm feeling friendly thoughts now about Bob, as I hope he is of me,
as we settle back to mull over what the preacher has to say.
Some words to guide our weary week more fruitfully
and maybe oil a few of the frictions.
Perhaps see God's hand in something where we hadn't.

Jesus didn't like the rabbinical hairsplitting, my wife tells me.
He liked it kept simple. Just two rules, she said:
Love God above all others. And love your neighbor as yourself.
I like it kept simple. Perhaps this is why I attend church.
Each Sunday I sit here and recollect the past week and try to keep it simple.
Finding what it means helps.
A friend used to say, "People are simple creatures, really."
But they forget it. I forget it. Bob admits that he, at times, forgets it.

I DON'T KNOW WHY

Riding with the windows down after swimming
on a blistering day through downtown Parkersburg, West Virginia
with Janis Joplin screaming between crumbling brownstones
and shoestring business establishments
feels so free and of one piece
as to set my soul trilling.
I don't know why.

Walking my dog in the midday heat, in stained linens,
wearing a straw hat and sweat streaked glasses
watching the slight breeze ruffle the leaves
and disorganize the grasses…
keeps me interested.
I don't know why.

My own dog lies flopped in the sunlight staring vacantly.
Next door, the dog howls as if in mourning.
Outside a dark car silhouette passes.
And it feels like midday twilight…
I don't know why.

MY SON SAYS I'M WEIRD; WON'T BRING HIS FRIENDS BY

I'm fascinated by wandering…
Being lost is the closest I've come to my vision.
Johnny Appleseed was my boyhood hero,
then Woody Guthrie, Moliere…
Hank Williams wandered in to suffer there somewhere.

Imagination is something which should be shared… very sparingly.
Trust me! Each little thought is as a ghost materialized
and too much is spooks redundant.
Plato's cave shadows dancing in the head's eye lights,
and playing peekaboo from behind the pupils
alerts people!
that there is a restless impatience -
perhaps, with them.

I wander everywhere:
in my head, across terrain,
even around the home.
Name those little towns in West Virginia
inaccessible except by gnarled roads
through endless forest lined hollers,
down cricks,
threading ridges.
They call to me as if ghouls.
I wander into the garage,
as if guided by an unseen force.
Start the car.

DINNER

“Take what you want and then pass it.
Leave some for others.”

I enjoy watching my son eat
through the dinner caterwaul.
He’s quiet and focused
like a boy with a history.
Enjoying his hamburger
as things that have gone well,
and his veggies
as things that need work.
That bully gets his potato mashed
and adds a little catsup to the plate.
And he drinks his milk all the way down.
‘Strong bones and add a little height,’ he’s thinking.

EARLY BIRD

The fruits of a father's discipline
are hard to forgo.
They will sit in the back of your mind
like the scowl of a discharged veteran.

In the hushed early morning, the neighbors heading to work
notice that odd fellow scribbling
sitting on his porch with just the birds,
long shadows and a few sprinklers turning.

I told my son, no one sleeps around here later than ten.
Any later and we're housing hoodlums and bums.
Good people go to bed - or failing that
still wake up on time, like fish, to get the chum.

"Today, son, is just scaffolding for tomorrow
and so forth, and so on."

A poet selects his words carefully for those he loves.

"Dreams, like worms," my pen spirals,
"digest yesterday's events in slow peristaltic action,
to create the scat from which to track your coming destiny.
But you must rise; you must awake!"

"Dad, you make no sense."

"If you can discipline yourself son,
you control the world."
. . .
The early bird gets the worm!"
I toss my arms.

And then a bird flew up yard
with a white grub in his beak, wriggling.

"Look!" I smiled.
"The prophecy is fulfilled."

HOW WILL I KNOW WHEN I SEE GOD?

Will I be buttering my toast,
when the toast will rise
from under my knife?
Will it be like the dream I had?
Will slugs reveal who they used to be?
Will every planet, all the asteroids (plus a lot of space debris) align?

I suppose,
My dog will desert me and run to His side.
My car won't run. And when I visit the mechanic,
He will glow.
And when I pee outside in the dirt,
I will see His face.

Like celebrity, He will assume I recognize Him.
He'll tell me He loves me, and I'll believe.
I will doubt everything else.
My wife will say, "I told you so."
My dog, sitting at His side, will speak Latin.
He will look like my son.

DAY WITH A COLD

My head is over stuffed,
with drubbed thought.

Staggering through a forest of coughing,
wheezing, sneezing…
My prescription:
Don't bother,
Belch if it helps.

I feel like breakfast for millions;
passing time like an atomic clock, slowly degrading;
sneezed adrift as a dandelion's seed.

PSYCHOLOGICAL PROJECTION

The Chinese woman boarding my bus
would never pay the complete fare.
She believed the Metro was cheating.

As I tried to quietly reason with my son,
he kept shouting that I should, "Stop yelling!"
And now at the pool,
what has gotten into *it*?

My first lap was silk sheets.
The waters parted so clean.
Then, pushing further,
I feel suddenly mortal -
as if in soaked clothes
and fighting for survival.

OUR OLD DOG
(CURLED IN SOME NEW POSITION)

His ears daydream.
He barks at poltergeists
who shuffle upstairs.

When he dies, my son
wants another just like him.
That's a pretty good testament,
I'd say.

The cat will miss our dog,
but like a wife
will go on living
marking off the years, alone.

Touch doesn't grow old.
Touch doesn't age, apparently.
He's ninety-one and when
we lie nudging,
even a nearby clatter
won't uproot his calm.

He ignores the table talk,
the TV chatter.
He snoozes better than ever
curled in some spiritual position
newborn as a nest of hairless mice.

WHAT THE DEER THINK

The yellow fawn in the blue-leafed grove stares,
its thought awash in a starburst of particulars.
A droplet of the drizzle springboards from leaf to forest floor
and the fawn blinks.
Perhaps it's waiting for something to appear.
Perhaps the fawn doesn't know what it's doing?
I don't know what I'm doing.

Perhaps it's waiting to see what will move and what won't,
to resolve background from foreground,
…movement from volition
to see desire spring from will.
Perhaps the fawn is waiting for something like itself, to see.
And he'll wait just as long as it would the other
and then move off, to wait elsewhere.
Just as long as I'll suffer this poem to emerge
and then move off.

I'M FORGETTING THINGS IN MY DREAMS

The other night my dream was proceeding
when I forgot where I was.
Friday, I wandered about the whole night
feeling I'd forgotten something too.
Spent a lot of time retracing my footsteps Tuesday,
then couldn't remember what I was looking for.

For example, I spent the whole of this past night trying to remember…
Tried every trick, even woke up to consider…
visualized everything around the vacancy
hoping for it to pop up like a rabbit…
went back to sleep.
And in the end, it was my left sock -
which had nothing to do with anything!
and barely worth noting.

Oddly, in dreams, I've never misplaced my glasses or hearing aids,
though I have lost my dog from time to time.

In dreams, I seem to forget my manners,
forget to arrive on time,
but remember a host of transgressions
and that all-over enveloping feel
of blushing, impermissible shame.

CUT WOOD AND HAUL WATER
(Written as if Translated from the Chinese)

When an idea struck,
the poet, Li Po,
set his buckets and picked up his pen.

When an idea struck the Emperor,
he was much too taken with national affairs
to bother with
more than a scribble.

After his death, boxes of these notes were found,
many indecipherable or plain:
"the snow falls",
"the crane's wings are white".

Indeed, it does
and they are,
were all his historians could add.

NINE MEN DESCRIBE LOVE
(after the Chinese proverb of nine blind wise men describing an elephant)

The first said, I haven't a clue as to what love is.

The fly flies.
The raindrop falls.
It is enough, said Dim San,
that I feel it daily.

While Bin Wang confessed
that throughout his love
he'd been apt to ask,
if there might have been others
more suited to her task.

Tan Wu had known women who loved him,
praised him, sung his genius.
Save one, who he literally could not leave alone!
Out along the plum blossom trail,
the game warden pursued her.
And in the hilltop shrine, the manager had waited patiently
until he'd gone to the john.

Yang Chou said it was as if time itself were imprisoned by the
boredom of it
after the thrill was gone.

Lee Wong could not fathom why anyone would not like his wife.
Though he did add that
"She can really piss me off!"

Inevitably, sighed Tu Fu,
their ass grows,
their teeth yellow,
their feet grow ugly knobs
and their leathery skin can no longer conjure
the golden boy I hold within.

Like a jellyfish floating free,
happenstance will swim right into it.
Love, love, love… I hate talking about it,
replied Fu Tam.

Yuan Fu was so obsessed,
he couldn't speak,
couldn't think.
Couldn't breathe.

VANISH

The rusted sign
"Home of the 1956 Hornets, State Basketball Champions."
swings from one hinge.
A granite statue covered in bird droppings
of the "Winning Shot"
points up the road.

Lying in bed on an upstairs floor,
up the creaking steps in an old house,
is a place to vanish,
a place slowly losing its human residue.

Lying on my back,
my eyes following the cracks,
I discern the lack of audience.
First it was the people,
now the spirits too
are drifting away.

The three story, brick bank stands abandoned on the town's square.
I see the open vault through dirty windows, completely emptied.
This next scene calls for period extras
to turn in concert as if coming to some great realization!

…and then head out in a growing crowd,
as if off to a warm, glowing Heaven,
leaving their picturesque past like leaves falling -
at first one by one, and then in clotted groups
who gather silhouetted in the setting sun
to say a few last words at the crossroads.

OUR BUTLERS

Feet,
with their ten little articulators,
are available for assignations
or as go-betweens.

Rarely targeted as pimps,
feet, ironically, are often portrayed as
foundational to tradition.

But they may play 'footsie'
or exchange warm messages
and yearnings for sexual gratification -
such as being stroked on the calf -
while betraying nothing.

As formerly dressed introverts
they prefer to hide in shined shoes
and underneath of tables, desks and counters.

Left foot, right foot,
conscripted together,
barracked together,

feet do not inspire
but perform without complaint.
No one wants to hear from them.

ALPHABET POEM

A bee can do exquisite flight gyrations,
hive integration, journeys, kinetic limb manipulations,
no problem! Questions?
(Next up) Ralph Stevens talks up
vibrator women, x-rated yahoos, zombies...

LIME IN MY BEER

Sitting on the front porch on a sunny summer afternoon as I am currently
has been my great life's goal, now accomplished.
With beer in hand, I'll add.
The placement of every detail has been much thought out.
No rough decisions would do it,
rather a gradual silting
stabilizing firmly as a river delta.
If lives were a house, I suppose mine would be of adobe
with friendships, cost-free as straw,
used as a binder for resilience and insulation.
You may have seen the article about me in "Sedimentary Living".

I enjoy a lime beer following my afternoon walk
by the old homes with their groomed lawns stretching down
towards the banks of Ol' Muddy's sister.
Now and then a body will wash up which had disappeared months before.
Someone never made it home in February, but wash up now in May.

I stroll about in linen taking my measure
with the lime in the beer as a bit of summer added:
sunny afternoon times blocked out for drifting
mixed generously with nodding off and thoughts wandering,
whole narratives moving overseas.

My porch elevates me as much as needed
so that whoever passes is poised to listen.
Which is the big take-away; the point I am pressing:
the provision of services unwittingly. There's the fly's ointment.
Preparing that empty space and letting nature fill in
like mom, like gravity, serving all of us quite intimately.

THE GOOD GARDNER

I would think that the Gardener might be the First
and near Universal Sign of the Enlightenment:
whereas, the Apple being bit - the Snake is beaten back!
Sweat and Labor will invariably win out!
That's the message the Good Gardener sends us.
God working through us, as it were…
Virtue and Success being His reward,
and the two, so entwined, form an intoxicating couple.

JUST A HEARTBEAT, THAT OLDE QUOTIDIAN

Then there's ambition.
We're all the start of something…
and it's hard to sit still,
as we haven't the time, really.

What with everything reaching…
flourishing,
crawling, creeping…
It's so hard,
the constant re-imagining
of this which is what's so pressing.

Always looming.
Always
Forever
Passing.

HOW THINGS WENT SO WRONG

To become one with the keening spirits
perspective is the first to fly,
as your own talent divests you.
The branches of the hustle twist in and out.
Order vanishes into an ineffable abyss processing, processing…
Dodges, hook-ups, scenarios, pitches, ploys and propositions
proliferate and crawl about like newly-hatched spiders.
All is tactics and ruses.
And this is where it starts to get creepy.

Smear your tears up and down those empty halls
rather than pay the high price of auditoriums.
Sooner or later that audience
which you found so prescient -
(who found *you*, once they've taken note) -
it's necessary to pay them.
(They've people everywhere.)

A FINE, WELL CONCEIVED POEM WOULD HAVE LOOKED GOOD HERE

Some crepe should be draped along the page bottom,
hung on the left and on the right margin,
leave the page gutter as is please and manage as best you can
this vacant poet's vicarage.
'Cause I'm short of verbiage.
There's been a death in my oeuvre.

A lovely, well-conceived poem could have really been ravished here.
As I had been hoping to meet my Muse in some mental
assignation…
with you and I - the writer and reader
sharing a rare flight of minds over all Elysium!
with assonance and dissonance in - hex a syllabic - the full tantric
position.

But, it seems, the nature of her Nature today not to bother, or
whatnot.
Creating a spot for your Muse can be like clearing a room.
You get an awful lot carted off just to find nothing there.
And it seems the nature of her Nature today not to bother,
as she's been fixing her hair and nails, scraping her corns,
…or whatever.

HER ANGER

A cackling hag dancing barefoot in the woods,
tired of being lied to, put down, being made fun of,
experienced a figure of darkness passing through her
and fumbling for her knife, woke up with bloody hands.

Spiders of revulsion, a fire burning in her belly,
that venom soaked kiss was her snapped pencil, her crushed cigarette.
His head thumping against a tattered hole in a burlap sack,
held in the tentacles of an octopus, was her anger.

- Sacred Way Poets
(phrases assembled by member Carl Nelson)

GOOD MAGIC

In the back of the book,
between the footnotes,
looking like a dropped comma,
happiness is the white wyrm, an unnatural chant.

Along the River of Po,
in the canal where corpses
rise like lilies,
lovely nyads
slender and deep
keep the travelers
off the reef.

Hints of sun
fringe clouds of gray,
winnow golden apples
on a morning lawn,
and circle corn flowers
'round the yard
and out the gate.

- from a collection of lines written by The Sacred Way Poets

THE FOLKS AROUND HERE

She said, "My great grandfather's a murderer.
He fought in the Civil War for the Union,
came back to Belpre to work in the butcher shop
where he argued with a colored man,
killed him with a meat cleaver,
then ran away to North Carolina,
where he led a successful life."

"Then my grandfather found a man making love to his wife in an apple orchard
and killed *him*.
He ran away to Colorado."

I asked if her father had murdered anyone.
"No," she said.
"But my mother confronted him once about an affair he'd had in Columbus.
"She's dead," he said emphatically.
And told her to never speak of it again,
" …ever."

Her own husband tried to shoot her three times.
The first time
"he shot his foot".
You'd have thought that would have cooled his jets.
But the second time, the gun was deflected by her arm
as she turned away.
The third time,
he had the gun pressed right into her abdomen.
"But it didn't fire."

He was an alcoholic and eventually she returned
to find him dead and stiffening
on the sofa.
I asked her if she had ever killed anyone.
"Not yet," she said.

WE LEAVE A GOOD CHUNK OF WHAT AILS US IN HIS HANDS

The stories you pick up here still have some earth on them.
The red grit gets tracked everywhere. Tongues wag.
The West is new and fresh and beautiful, but…
my home is here. My work's here.

We're largely isolated and think of the government, when we have to,
as the Jews thought of the Czar:
"May the Lord bless and keep the Czar,
far away from us."*

A train crosses the river regularly pulling its litter
of coal and tanker cars full of synthetic carbon polymer
from vats webbed in a mesh of pipes and flaming stacks upriver.
Sports caps, coveralls, boots and pick-ups are worn in small to extra
large sizes.
Concrete and UPS truck drivers play the fiddle and mandolin
in shotgun styled clubs, nights and weekends.
Pickers come from small towns along the Ohio and deep into West
Virginia.
Fishing, hunting, sports and 'mudding' are predominant activities.
And the people, deep in the forests here, sit on porches meditating.
They open doors, nod recognition, and don't shove.
They're oddly meek, leaving the worst to God's benevolence,
and the best to God's benevolence, and unlike progressives,
we leave a big chunk of what ails us in His hands.

* from, *Fiddler on the Roof*

POET IN APPALACHIA

When you phone hill folk,
they won't answer.
And when you knock,
they'll hide in the back.

They're often shy and a little wary.
'Why would anyone be comin' clear out here?'
is a natural wonder - and a worry.

The hills and the hollers,
their shale sides slippery with leaves,
and endless oaks of unbroken woods
make it hard to take a bearing
and form a natural barrier.

Find some nest of relations and you'll be embedded,
free to say your forbidden words,
spout your curious thoughts,
even get drunk and
carve them into trees.

If your words don't fit their thinking,
they may laugh.
But they'll adjust to you
as a rather odd outsider
but nevertheless, kin.

PLAYING CARDS

My mother-in-law taught us the game of Cinch
and left us a taste for Euchre,
mentally disabling as moonshine
with rules twisted as back roads
ensnared in morning glory.

Cinch is about four games played at once.
There is high, low, Jack and game,
plus the question of whether or not you made bid -
or were 'set'.
The Jack might appear or not.
And you could trump anything,
anytime, no matter. And then,
even if you took the trick -
the low card goes to whoever played it.

My father-in-law cannot remember if he's just 'et dinner,
but his card playing's shrewd as ever.
We silenced the TV, laughed about the poor family beagle,
and chatted about the relations "way back on Sally's backbone,
that ridge just north of Fish Crick holler",
with odd names like "Zip" and "Corny",
and about this fellow in my father-in-law's dorm at college,
"who'd eat anything - and *everything* - you put in front of him.
And yeah. The guy was *BIG*."

THE SOULS OF CHRISTMAS CREATIONS ESCAPE TO ANIMATE STRANGERS

I know I'm always stirred when the cosmos grips me
like kids at Christmas
wandering in a new snowfall and remarking
to whoever's there to hear.

He circled me twice. "You get that for Christmas?"
"Bought it for myself. It was a present for myself," he said,
revolving.
He rode a red mountain bike
on larger tires than I'd ever seen…
"If I hit one of those cracks in the sidewalk? Don't even feel it."
He spiraled, while continuing to talk.
"I can't walk. It hurts my ankles. I have type two diabetes."
Then, pulling out, "I've lost 60 pounds," he called back.

Meanwhile, a fellow on a shiny silver Harley drives through,
and then back again on his way, the other way, still smiling
that early Christmas afternoon while I was out walking.
The outdoor lights still hung, some sagging,
and the comic, inflatable creations were puddles of fabric.

NO SEE UMS

Certainly not the size of the wasp, horse fly or even mosquito -
there is a bug with almost no presence.
They're spoilers whose only merit is annoyance.
Petulance is the mood they spread,
destroying the pleasure of your chair, book or lemonade.

Some think they *don't* exist, but as a folk legend.
They have been described variously as if a cloud of miniscule UFOs,
or as a generalized symptom complex found in highly susceptible,
affected individuals
whose affliction presents itself most often as these subjects sit on
porches
drinking tea or 'spirits', discussing events.

For no apparent reason, it has been noted,
the natives of these portions of the country will hit themselves,
first one, and then progressively all the others
in a sort of contagion, swatting, self abusing,
while cursing a cloud of petulant, pissy '*spirits*' called
"no see 'ums".

Circulating in a non-haze of irascible sensation -
rather like wading through a jelly fish cluster
they have been described.

DAY SHIFT

The pale, skinny woman sucks a cigarette
while talking on the phone and examining a fingernail.
She honks at the license plate in front when the light turns,
then veers abruptly,
casts a hard stare
and tosses curses like rocks.

The side mirror hangs off the door and the glass is cracked.
The passenger window has had a fairly large cinder block bounced off it.
Cardboard covers another. The trunk is wired shut.
The car is a flat rust color, and the bumper was for Humphrey.

At work she's a jejune laundress
struck dumb by the piles of it
soiled in every conceivable way,
wadded in a ball or just left -
oppressing her life, fattening itself on her best qualities,
working her fragile beauties like dumb brutes or plow horses.
Until she's "just about had it" for several days now,
with forever to go.

ZUCCHINIS

"Poetry and zucchinis are the two most overproduced commodities in America."
- Judson Jerome, poet/ columnist

My neighbor leaves zucchinis on my porch.
He says the recent rains have made them flourish.
If he keeps it up, I'm going to start leaving poems on his.

Others find my neighbor's gesture normal, even gracious,
while finding *me* odd. Perhaps even presumptuous
and toss my poems,
or adversely, read them obsessively,
as if to say, "What do you imply?"

Is there something suspicious about poetry?
Or something in a sun-ripened zucchini
which causes all boats to rise?

Is there something grown under moonlight
which speaks of illicit understanding?
Something which eludes,
speaking from both sides of the word, the page,
the mouth,
denied the public's best estimate,
and undermining wherever like a mole?

"Here," I might as well say,
"I thought I'd offer you a bit of what's lurking."
While they react as if I've handed them a snake.

IN A PIN HOLE

I'm getting old looking into my mirror,
and it's disturbing staring into my demise,
taking the long look to where the vanishing point resides.
I'm going out with the telephone poles and the train tracks.
Headed to where there is nowhere left to go.
No up or down. No sideways.

All drawing students must learn perspective.
They must learn to draft eternity into everything.
Put the hereafter in there too.
Just a pin hole is enough for mastery.

All of this, all of our creation
ends up no larger than a speck.
While love and affection flood back and forth,
rise and fall as if a tide pool,
across an absence.

As my life ends, a toad hops…
bouncing sounds gradually coming to a stop.

ABOUT THE AUTHOR

"To many hard won epiphanies and aha! moments without practical results have left an empty shell of this artist."
- Bogus Reviews

Carl Nelson spent twenty years in the Seattle theater community, during which time he wrote and produced plays, directed others, and performed whenever the talent was missing but a body still needed. Before that he did stand-up comedy.

The author now lives in Belpre, Ohio where he moseys about.

www.ingramcontent.com/pod-product-compliance
Lightning Source LLC
Chambersburg PA
CBHW060623030426
42337CB00018B/3167

* 9 7 8 0 6 9 2 6 3 8 9 5 8 *